All The Grief I Ever Knew

Loz Holdy

BookLeaf
Publishing

Presentation by *BookLeaf Publishing*

Web: www.bookleafpub.com

E-mail: info@bookleafpub.com

ISBN: 9789357440219

First edition 2023

*Richard Latcham, admiration spans the
decades, the motorways, those river days.
you have known, lost and written as I have.
deeper, harder and better respectively.*

ACKNOWLEDGEMENT

Thanks without end to Matty. I had to write this first, but really my heart has written All The Love You Ever Gave since knowing you these sixteen years.

To Kaff. So much of it all has been made possible with you, your humour, your jibing, your love.

And Mum. without you I would not be here, would not know Love. The biggest grief of all is to think that one day will we will say goodbye. For now.

PREFACE

At it's core this anthology seeks to explore the ephemeral nature of life and the permanence of its loss through the senses of a woman aged 16 to 38 and all the years in-between.

Suddenly.

Bursting forth swallows scatter,
The tree so predictable her ways,
You;
Ever moving,
Never grounded.

You strike the core of man,
Nature;
Patterns murmur through clouded hearts.
You become us,
Shape our lives,
Like no other.

Oh Holy Night

The day he died,
You rolled,
I cried.
Death stung,
No joy came that mourning.

Night took not only him,
Unfurled you rose,
Gone.
But ever looking on.

A broken mind,
A weeping wound,
Full.
of fury,
Tom.

Oh silent night,
Where is the dawn?
Will you weep with those who mourn?

Merry Go Mothering

Call it what you like,
Stuck on the merry go round,
Unable to dismount the horse of feeling,
To which I do not belong.
Unable to escape to the bench of apathy,
In the corner of the park,
Where I wish I to be Spectator.

Instead stuck,
On this perfect stallion of smiles,
Sorrowful inside.
Onlookers,
Expectant for their turn,
Ignorant.

Those in front can no longer see me,
Though we were friends when we got on,
Estranged we will be when we alight.
From behind,
friends who do see,
Can't quite reach,
To help,
Me,
Pause,

The conductor?
He's on a break.

No-one is answering my desperate pleas
For a moment's rest.

The Soul Rants What It Rants

I crave simplicity
Beauty
Longevity of mind!

Where does one turn to
Can anyone find
The solution to this
Problem
Of modernity

So filled
with
Anxiety,
Stupidity
Of
Far,
Too,
Much?

Teenage Angst 2001

Pencils,
Scrawling my soul,
Crossing the bridges,
Bearing the bruises.

Running on eggshells,
Blisters from new heels,
Mud on the dance floor,
Mud on the dance floor,

I should sing you this song,
So you can belong,
To something you dream of,
So you won't feel wronged,
But it's all just pencils and paper,
Scratching my soul,
Crossing old bridges,
With too many bruises.

All that's left is the eggshells,
You've run out of tears,
Your blisters are bleeding,
And singing this kills,
There's mud on the dancefloor,
And blood on your sleeves,

Your soul searching finishes,
With pencil and paper.
Scrawling,
The End.

How would you like this to end?

Over the top
Above the parapet
Stick
Up
Your head.

Excessive
Inordinate
Extreme
Above and beyond,
Just to be seen.

Shut up,
Sit down,
Don't
make
A sound.

Dissolution of a Marriage

The ode of time,
Forget me not I pray,
Deleted by your fantasies,
Discovering no mysteries.
Nothing new lies in this heat
Though it burns hotter than before,
Melting you but not your heart.

Rising tides of uncertainty,
Floods delete our memories,
Floundering we in the puddles now,
For this heart burns hotter still,
And you forgot the truth
Of us.

I.B.Done with this shit

This is Crohn's
Its not all poo on the loo
In the middle of the night
Its needles and MRI's
Tears and heavy sighs
Constant paint
Progress down the drain
It goes into the bones
Into the eyes
Pervades every part of a healthy life
Joy, turning to strife!
Striving for health
Driven to bedrest
Changing the diet, cutting out food
Full of low mood
Low nutrition
Low iron
High inflammation
Stealing joy
Crohns is shit
Its utterly crap
I be done with it.

Retreat

Silence forces into submission,
The pain that would rather have taken refuge,
In the comfort of screaming,
The liberation of conversation,
The joy of singing

Things That Go Ache In The Night

Body,
Womb,
Soul.

Eyes,
Heart,
Cries.

Stay Positive

Luck of the plucky
Young
Egg.
Cracked and broken
Open
My soul
To hospital tiles
Poured out.
Not so lucky now.

Oi Greys

Hark!
The forest floor lays on a rich bounty of greed
for you,
Grey fur and yellow teeth
Boundless in your consumption!
You nothing nothing of mercy
Or restraint
You have come in droves!
Killed my comrades
With writhing and foaming
You foreigners here!
Your drays don't belong among our kind.

Dear Reds,

We are the survivors!
Dont hate on us,
The fittest
Don't demonise us!
We aren't out to kill you,
Don't seek to destroy you,
We can't help that we're
Better than,
Faster than,
Fitter than,
Like prisoners of fancy,
Look upon, specimens in captivity
Revered.
In our freedom now,
Feared.
Are ailments are not a weapon,
We never unleashed with,
Intension!

Man or woe-man as they're sometimes known,
Stole your lands,
Stole your freedom to roam.
The wander now to enjoy what is left of you,
They seek to destroy us now too!

Yours, Grey.

To Whom This May Concern,

Can you see red for us?
Were hanging by a thread
Like so many others,
Our homes now lay scattered,
Shattered,
Obliterated.

Woe-man and woe-men,
Need to change for us,
Fight for us,
Die to their greed for us!
Plead for us,
Please,
For us,
See Red.

Grim

You flood our barren lands
Despite you
New life Springs
Ever hopeful,
Always knowing
You Will come again

Sand Bags and Prayer Flags

The willow weeps
For time will keep
No memory
Of your roots
Your sacrifice
So polarised
And we will surely miss the view

Take a Hike

Grief in the darkness
Nothing remains well lit here
Limen Of vision.

Your DNA forever In My Mind

Mourn with those who miscarry
Grieve with those bleed

Drowning we in puddles,

And you

can't hold

the grief of it.

Psalm 139. Never

You did not hold on,
You did not hold form,
Never Born,
The one,
In four,
No blanket will be made
Now,
He just
Stopped,
      Knitting.

Recovering Perfectionist

Oh grief!
 In bed,
 Still in my head,
Urge myself to move.

Arise!

Lack the lark,
The joy, the song,
Of getting it all wrong,
But having done it anyway.

The Place You Now Inhabit

The Everyday
You now
In my
Every Movements
Objects touched
The places unseen.
Our bed
My bed!
Toothbrush
The Toaster
Burning Hotter
Crisp my desire
To feel.
You.
Move.
Your pillow
My teacup
The Cafetiere
That smirk you gave
The smell of your hair.
You now
In my every Hope.

Messages in the mirror
Now wishes in the shower

I live in this egg box
Of broken dreams
Shells left
Pain unspoken
Inhabit
Me.
Please
Depart not our memories

You there in their smiles
The shape of their frame
They grow
And I know
They'll not be the same
Off - you - sprang
Adventures
Unknown

Open the oven
Air Fryer
Look in the sink
Thrust down the dishwasher door
Tears pour
On the floor.
The engine purrs
The Dog whimpers
Children howl
How we used to laugh
At the scamper of paws

And the patter of tiny feet we made
Those intimate moments
Now cast only in my mind
Sounds soured
silencing joys

Eat up
Waste not
Hunger
Evades
Us
All
Cupcake cases
Suits in wardrobes
Running shoes
And those brightly coloured watch straps
All spaces void of you.
Soft arms of hoodies
Empty bookshelves
Your mind full
I got rid of them all
Pained to say goodbye
To the wonder you held so tenderly
Hold.
Me.
Tenderly.
Flip flops
With socks
Taking out the bags,

Rubbish was a boy job
Now its all my job
My love
My passion
My zeal
Ripped in a moment
A flash

Ripples in the sheets
Your body
Your skin, your tone
Your life of wisdom
Gone

Peer into the place you now inhabit
My eggcup
My shoe
This house
Our home
Cant stop thinking
Switch off the whirring
Skin crawling
Pen scrawling
Misery
Every day
You now
In my
Every day.